Cognitive, Behavioral Therapy

You Can Use Without a Therapist

By

Virginia Hansen, MSW

Foreword

It is a rare occurrence to find a book that has the potential to change a person's life. "Cognitive Behavioral Therapy, You Can Use Without a Therapist" is one of those books. Virginia Hansen MSW introduces Cognitive Behavioral Therapy in a straight forward manner in this easy-to-use book filled with exercises anyone can do to make concrete changes and see results quickly.

Virginia Hansen's approach is a reflexion of her unique blend of experience, both on personal and professional levels. I have been witness to the warmth, focus, and ease she brings to relationships with her clients. She understands the importance of taking an active role in one's own life changes. The empowerment that comes with taking steps to a better life is without a price. With "Cognitive Behavioral Therapy, You Can Use Without a Therapist" the reader has the tools in their own hands.

Jennifer Goliger

Cognitive, Behavioral Therapy
What it is and How it Works

Cognitive Behavioral Therapy assumes that beliefs, ideas, emotions and behavior are interconnected (Donohue & Fisher,2006) and that a person's perception of an event determines the person's feelings and behavior (Leahy,2003). Cognitive Behavioral Therapy is restructuring thoughts, feelings and behavior.

The theory behind Cognitive Behavioral Therapy (CBT) reasons that what one thinks controls what one feels and what one feels controls how one behaves (or how one acts or reacts).

THOUGHT → EMOTIONS →BEHAVIOR

According to the Cognitive Behavioral theory, if you can change your thoughts, you can change your emotions, thus changing your behavior.

CBT is an eclectic therapy which consists of several therapies. These therapies have similar characteristics which include: cognitive model of emotional response, time limiting, collaboration between the client and the therapist, it is structured and directive, it is based on the educational model that behavior is learned, it uses homework for clients and it uses Socrates logic based method of questioning and Aristotle's method of categorizing information about the world (Leahy, 2003).

CBT model therapies include: Cognitive Therapy (CT), Prolonged Exposure (PE), Dialectical Behavioral Therapy (DBT), Solution Focus Therapy, Narrative Therapy, Eye Movement Therapy, Cognitive Processing Therapy (CPT), and Behavioral Therapy.

The two major therapies we will focus on are behavioral therapy and cognitive therapy. Both of these therapies are backed up by Solution Focus Therapy. Once you understand these two therapies, you will better understand Cognitive Behavioral Therapy (CBT).

Behavior Therapy was born in the United States. It is the child of Skinner. He redefined family behavior learning (Early). Behavioral Therapy focuses on operant conditioning, modeling and verbal information. Behavioral Therapy considers behavior as inclusive of everything people do, think, feel and respond

(Lineman & Wagner). The assumption of BT is that Behavior is a product of learning. We are both the product and the producer of our environment.

Cognitive Therapy is based on George Kelly's 1955 model of "man as scientist." This means that people can identify their own beliefs and test them. Beck and Emery took this model (1995) and molded it into the cognitive theory that focused on a person's ability for scientific thinking that tests a belief by examining how it could be proven wrong,

The goal of CBT is to approach problems by stressing the importance of identifying patterns of thinking, rather than focusing on the expression of emotion, although emotion is an important wealth of information.

CBT is based on Beck's 1995 Cognitive Therapy, Meichenbaum's 1994 Cognitive Behavioral Therapy, and Ellis's 1996 Rational Emotive Behavior Therapy. It combines Behavioral Therapy from the 1950's with the Cognitive Therapy of the 1960's.

Changing your thoughts from negative to positive is not always easy and does not mean that you take on a Pollyanna approach. (1st person singular and turns into 1st person plural.) What it means is that we don't sweat the small stuff. We exchange the energy and time wasted dwelling on what we can't do and focus it on what we can. Leahy warns that it is important that one does not become a cheerleader for positive thinking. It should not be a process for bolstering defenses or doubt the power of positive thinking.

Positive thought can make it possible to love who you are and to silence those negative voices that you have carried around with you throughout your life. For years of believing that you do not possess the ability that others seem to have. You feel you have fall short of the bar set by society. You can finally change those beliefs and concentrate on the realistic bar that you can finally see before you. This is the bar of our acceptance of who we really are and the destruction of the negative thoughts and emotions that we have lived with for so long. We can change our thoughts, our emotions and our behavior. We can change our thought patterns at any time during the cycle.

THE KEY TO CHANGE IS CAREFUL SELF OBSERVATION

Negative Thought→ Negative Emotions→ Negative Behavior
↓ ↓ ↓
↓ ← ←
Positive Thought → Positive Emotion → Positive Behavior

Changing the thought patterns of a lifetime takes time and effort. Don't be discouraged. This life changing experience does not need to be stressful. Relax. Instead of making it a chore, make it fun. Let that be your first lesson in CBT. Have fun while changing your life.

You can move forward without having to look back.   We learn constantly throughout our lives. Consider that right now you see things differently than when you were ten years younger. You are the same person you were, only with more knowledge beneath your belt.   You are the best expert on your life experiences and the meaning of certain events in your life.   So as you take this journey, remember that it is time to remove "always" and "never" from your vocabulary. There are always exceptions. Remain flexible, nothing is set in stone.

ASSIGNMENT 1

Change takes careful self-observation. This can be done with adherence to homework. Obtain a notebook, which will be your journal/homework book. The first homework assignment is to write down three things each night that you like about yourself. Keep it simple. Don't justify or minimize. Do this for two weeks. You should have forty two entries at the end of two weeks. Do not replicate. Each day should have three separate and different entries and each days entries cannot be repeated in any other day. This may take some real work, especially if you have never thought that you were worth loving. On the last day read over your entries and celebrate the special person that you are discovering.

Solution Focus Therapy

Solution Focus was created using one way mirrors during therapy sessions at the Brief Therapy Center in Milwaukee by Steve de Shazer and others as they paid attention to the clients that seemed to be making progress . They discovered that the clients who made progress were those who identified goals for change. Solution Focus Therapy assumes that: (1) Clients are competent to co-plan their goals and know how to reach them, (2) That clients are the best judges about their own lives and the meanings of their experiences, (3) there is not necessarily a connection between the problem and a solution, (4) clients must do something different to make a change in their life, sometimes only a small change is enough. (5) If it isn't broken or it works, don't fix it.

Problems usually have more than one solution. You, as the best expert on your life, will select the best solution. No matter how bleak things are, environments contain resources. You have strengths that you can use to better your life. In Solution Focus Therapy (SFT) you focus on the solution rather than the problem. You build on strengths from past experiences. Remember, nothing is set in stone. With few exceptions nothing is "always or never". Be flexible and willing to look for different solutions or the solutions that have worked before.

ASSIGNMENT II

Think carefully about the following sentence: If you had a magic bullet to make things perfect - What would your world look like? What would be different?

Cognitive Therapy

Cognitive Therapy (CT) is based on George Kelly's 1955 model "man as scientist". This means that people can identify their own beliefs and test them. Beck and Emery took this model and molded it into the Cognitive Therapy. They did this by focusing on peoples ability for scientific thinking that tests a belief by examining how it could be proven wrong.

Cognitive Therapy is based on the view that stressful states are maintained by exaggerated ways of thinking. Stressors are cognition in emotion and schematic processing as the determining factor in information processing. CT's assumption is that how a person's interpretation of an event determines the emotions and behavior of that person. The purpose of CT is to achieve a cognitive approach to their problem by realizing and identifying patterns of thinking, rather than focusing on the emotion itself. To achieve an accurate and objective picture of the traumatic event and your role in it, focus on correcting faulty thinking that can lead to drawing faulty conclusions about your role in an event.

Cognitive Distortions

Beliefs are the most important part of CBT. They are what drives what people do and do not do. Clusters of thought create beliefs. Our beliefs can be distorted, creating false assumptions about ourselves and those around us. It is our perceptions that control our cognitive thought and thus our behavior. Changing those distortions can change our feelings about ourselves and this will change our behavior.

You can learn to identify automatic distortion or unrealistic thought patterns and challenge those irrational beliefs. In addition you will be able to do these things individually.

Some Cognitive Distortions

Mind Reading - You assume you know what people think without having sufficient evidence of their thoughts. (ie. "He thinks I'm stupid.")

The ability to read minds should be regulated to King Solomon. Since we don't know every bit of history about another person, their thoughts, mental state, or emotions, we cannot accurately read another person's mind. What someone may or may not think of us could be completely the opposite of what we think they are really thinking. It could also be exactly what we think however, the question remains... Did our perception create the thought?

Fortune Telling - You predict the outcome with the worse case scenario (ie. I will fail this test").

Since most of us only have two eyes, with the third future looking eye missing, we would be erroneous to think that we can predict the future outcome of most situations. Rather than predict the outcome, one can prepare for all outcomes, but consider this... is this probable or even important. Will predictions change anything? Maybe, maybe not.

Catastrophizing - You believe that what has happened or will happen will be so terrible that you won't be able to bear it. (ie. "It will be terrible to lose").

We believe that nothing but horrible things will happen. Our fear immobilizes us and we fail to try. We wait for the train wreck. Oops!!!

Labeling - You assign negative labels to yourself and others (ie. "I am the dumbest person in this room").

Labeling is something that you do over and over again until you have it down good and tight. It doesn't take long before the label is attached good and tight.

Discounting the positives - You trivialize positive accomplishments made by you or others. (ie. "It was too easy, therefore it wasn't an accomplishment" or "Anyone can do it and do it better")

Can't gracefully accept a compliment? Can't believe you are good at something? You think you were just lucky and you didn't really have any thing to do with your accomplishment

Negative Filter - You focus on the negative and seldom see the positive. (ie. "Everyone here doesn't like…").

Everything is out of kilter. Nothing about this is good. Sound familiar

Over generalizing - You perceive a global pattern of negativity on the basis of a single incident. (ie. "I always seem to fail").

Last month I failed an exam. Last week I lost at hearts. I always fail at whatever I do.

Dichotomous thinking - You perceive events or people in all or nothing terms. (ie. "I get rejected by everyone.").

 He didn't look up when I walked by. He hates me. She talked to Tom for ten minutes before she saw me standing there. What a snob.

Should's - You interpret events in terms of how things should be rather than simply focusing on what is (ie. " I should do well, but if not then I am a failure.").

Should's, should not's, could's and could not's, and ought to's and ought not's **SHOULD BE BANNED FROM THE ENGLISH LANGUAGE!!!!**

Personalizing - You attribute a disproportionate amount of blame for negative events to yourself and fail to see that certain events are also caused by others. (ie. "It was my fault that my marriage ended.").

It is a true gift that we take the burden of guilt onto our broad shoulders. It is not a gift. It has halted our ability to love ourselves and forgive ourselves and others. We do no one a great service by taking on their responsibilities for their action and accept them as our own.

Blaming - You focus on the other person as the source of your negative feeling and you refuse to take responsibility of changing yourself. (ie. "I lost because my parents caused all my problems.").

Blaming others will only block your ability to change your thoughts and Behavior. CBT, although it is intended or meant to change your negative thoughts, must be taken seriously and with honesty.

Unfair comparisons - You interpret events in terms of standards that are unrealistic by focusing primarily on others who do better than you and then judging yourself inferior in the comparison. (ie. He is more successful than me. I am a failure.").

Comparison is good when shopping or buying a car, insurance, etc., however; it is always a mistake to compare yourself with others.

Regret orientation - You focus on how you could have done better in the past rather than how you can do better now. (ie. "I should have tried harder, I might be better off if I had.").

You focus on what you **could or should** have done. Is it over? Then get rid of the **COULDA, SHOULDA, WOULDA.**

What if? - You ask a series of questions about "what if" something happens and the answers never satisfy you (ie. "What if I freeze up or something?").

What if the world ends tomorrow. What if, what if... Yeah, but what if? By this time you have wasted the chance and you will never know.

Emotional reasoning - You let your emotions guide your thinking. (ie. "My friend just left and I know that I will fail without him here.").

Emotions are a good thing, however they can control your thoughts and your behavior. Remember, your thoughts control your emotions which control your behavior. Use your thoughts to control your reasoning, and your emotions will follow through.

Inability to disconfirm - You reject any evidence or arguments that might contradict your negative thoughts. (ie. "I am unlovable." You reject any evidence that people like you. Or "That's not the real issue. There are deeper problems. There are other factors" Your thoughts cannot be refuted.).

Changing our way of looking at things can be difficult. Accepting that we are not what our negativity has told us we are is even more difficult. And if we have others feeding into this, it is even more so. We close up like a clam and nothing anyone says will make us open up. The only that can do that is you.

Judgment Focus - You view yourself, others and events in terms of black/white evaluation (good/ bad, superior/inferior) rather than simply describing, accepting or understanding. You are continually measuring yourself and other according to arbitrary standards and finding that you and other fall short. You are focused on the judgments of others as well as your own judgments of yourself. ("Look how successful she is. I am a failure".).

I always said, I would never make a good judge, because nothing is ever black and white with me. It doesn't help your chance of healing, if all you do is judge on strictly black and white and refuse to just accept what is. What good does it do to judge yourself? Do like feeling guilty? Do you need to take responsibility for something you have done or said? Then take the responsibility and then forgive yourself. Let go of the past and get on with your healing.

ASSIGNMENT III

Look at the list above. Identify which ones may apply to you. Don't try to analyze it, justify it or understand it. Just chose the ones you feel may apply to you or which ones strike a cord. Read them, that's all. Just read them and sit back and let it mingle and swarm or whatever it wants to do, but don't push it, don't analyze it and don't worry about it. This assignment is just simply to allow yourself to see something you may have not seen before and to let you begin to allow yourself a peaceful and gentle awakening.

Characteristic of CBT, CPT, BT and SF

The characteristics of the therapies listed is: (1) a cognitive model of emotional response, (2) briefer time limited, (3) Stoic philosophy (except CT), (4) it is structured and directive, (5) based on educational model (ie. learned behavior) and (6) requires homework. Because CBT looks forward and works on today, not looking back or reliving negative experiences, CBT has been useful in treating PTSD in both the military and civilian clients.

Remember you can change your irrational thoughts during any part of the process; at the point of negative thought, during negative emotion and before negative behavior. You can even change it after the negative behavior. It takes conscience thought and practice. Eventually you will usually be able to do it automatically.

Negative thought often is the fore runner of anxiety. It's okay to be afraid of something, but when it stops you from living a good and normal life, it is time to change the negative to the positive. Being anxious is like suffering in advance. Are you worried about what other people think? Then you are a prisoner of other people's thoughts.

Relaxation exercising, including breathing exercises and visualization exercises can help you relax and change the direction of your thoughts.

ASSIGNMENT IV

Do one of the breathing exercises and then do the visualization.

Breathing Exercise #1

Close your mouth and breath in slowly through your nose. Open your mouth and breathe out slowly, until all the air is pushed out of your lungs. Repeat.

Breathing Exercise #2

Breathe in through the nose to the count of four, hold the air for the count of four and breath out through the mouth for the count of four.

Visualization

Find a quiet place. You can listen to soft music or sounds of nature if you wish. Sit back or lay down and take three deep breaths (in through the nose, out through the mouth. Close your eyes. Now go into a world of your making in your mind. Make sure it is a quiet friendly place that you go to, not chaotic or busy, just quiet and peaceful. Look around you. Imagine the smells, the sounds and the feelings (such as the breeze or the feel of the sun on you face). This can be an imaginative place or a real place, but make it your place.

COGNITIVE BEHAVIORAL THERAPY

Combining the principles of CT, BT and SFT, Cognitive Behavioral therapy is looking foreword, finding solutions and changing our distorted beliefs. It assumes that thought creates emotions that create behavior, that create thought, etc., etc.

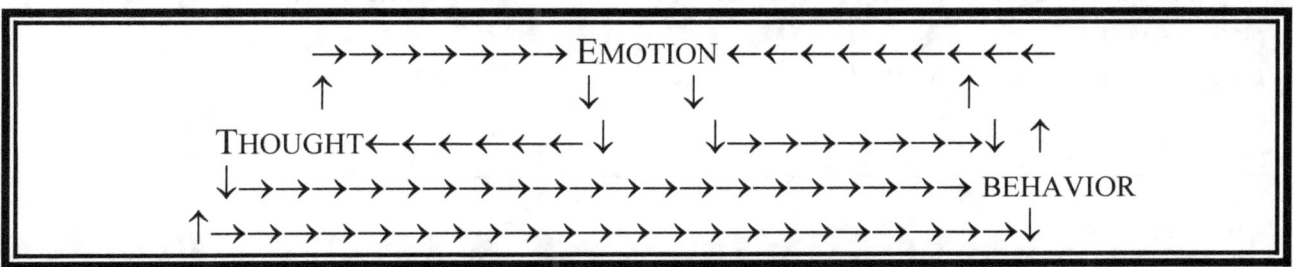

Why is a baseline important? It gives us information and helps us set goals that will change the way we are. Change needs self-observation.

The next couple of Assignments will concentrate on baselines and goals. You will be writing a contract, stating your rewards for meeting your goals and sub-goals. Your larger goal will have several smaller goals imbedded in it. Goals must be specific and realistic. Select a reward. It should be something you really enjoy and is under your control. It should be powerful to match the goal. It should be immediately available when you meet your goal.

ASSIGNMENT V

Make a list of pleasant activities - social - list two (2) people you would like to spend more time with, list two (2) places you would like to go, list two (2) things you would like to have, list four (4) foods or drinks that you like but seldom have, List two (2) activities you would like to do more often. Select three (3) from the lists you just made.

PLEASANT ACTIVITIES CONTRACT

My goal for the next week is to do at least _____ pleasant activities every day.

Each day that my daily total is _____, I will reward myself with

_____

_____

(smaller reward)

If I reach my goal five (5) days out of seven (7) during the next week; I will

reward myself with_____

_____

(bigger reward)

Signed_____ Date_____

Goal Met   Mon ____ Tues ____ Wed ____ Thurs _____ Fri _____ Sat _____ Sun _____

Goal Met   Mon ____ Tues ____ Wed ____ Thurs _____ Fri _____ Sat _____ Sun _____

Examples of Negative Thoughts

Check all that Apply:

_____ I'm confused

_____ There is no love in the world

_____ I am wasting my life

_____ I'm scared

_____ Nobody loves me

_____ I'll end up living all alone

_____ People don't consider friendship important anymore

_____ I don't have any patience

_____ What's the use?

_____ That was a dumb thing for me to do (or say)

_____ I'll probably be placed in a mental institution some day

_____ Anyone who thinks I'm nice, doesn't know the real me

_____ Life has no meaning

_____ I'm ugly

_____ I can't express my feelings

_____ I'll never find what I really want

_____ I'm not capable of loving anyone

_____ I am worthless

_____ It's all my fault

_____ Why do so many bad things happen to me?

_____ I can't think of anything that would be fun.

_____ I don't have what it takes to be successful

_____ I'll never get over this depression.

Examples of Positive Thoughts

Check all that Apply:

_____ Life is interesting
_____ I really feel great
_____ I'm having fun
_____ I have great hopes for the future
_____ I think I can do a good job at this
_____ I have good self control
_____ I have enough time to accomplish the things I want to do in my life
_____ I like people
_____ People like me
_____ I have a good sense of humor
_____ There are some things I am very good at
_____ I'm pretty lucky
_____ I deserve to have good things happen
_____ I have some very good friends
_____ I can learn new skills to gain control of my mood
_____ I can find a solution for most of the problems that come up
_____ Other people think that I am fun to be with
_____ I'm a good listener
_____ I'm okay the way I am
_____ Even if things don't always go my way, I'll live through it
_____ I have some skills (sports, reading, art, music, etc.) that I'm good at
_____ I'm doing alright
_____ Even though it is a rainy day, I will keep myself busy.
_____ I often receive compliments for doing something well

EXAMPLES OF PLEASANT EVENTS

1. Soaking in the bathtub
2. Planning your career.
3. Going on vacation
4. Collecting things (coins, shells, etc.)
5. Relaxing
6. Going to a movie in the middle of the week.
7. Jogging, walking
8. Listening to music
9. Buying household items
10. Lying in the sun
11. Laughing
12. Reading
13. Hobbies
14. Spending the evening with friends
15. Gambling
16. Eating
17. Practicing Karate, Judo, etc.
18. Repairing things around the house.
19. Working on car
20. Having quiet evening
21. Taking care of plants
22. Swimming
23. Exercising
24. Painting, drawing
25. Playing golf
26. Playing basketball, softball, etc.
27. Flying kites
28. Riding motorbike
29. Camping
30. Singing
31. Arranging flowers
32. Practicing religion (going to church, praying, etc)
33. Going to the beach
34. Going for a drive in the country
35. Gardening
36. Hiking
37. Traveling
38. Playing musical instruments

Why a Baseline?

A base line can help you identify negative thoughts and beliefs. It gives you a point to start from. Forming a Negative Baseline, you will want to have a set number of days seven or fourteen, and then you will want to identify the negative thought or belief, what words or instance activated it and how many times each day that you caught yourself using it.

A pleasant activity baseline will help you keep track of your pleasant activities and motivate you to include this in your daily life. It will also help you track your activities to help you fulfill your contract with yourself.

Assignment VI

Develop a negative thoughts baseline and a pleasant activities baseline. You can use the examples shown.

Example:

Negative Thoughts Baseline

Starting Date_____

DAY	NEGATIVE THOUGHT	ACTIVATING EVENT	NUMBER OF TIMES I CAUGHT MYSELF
1			
2			
3			
4			
5			
6			
7			

Example

BASELINE OF PLEASANT ACTIVITIES

ACTIVITIES   DAYS

ACTIVITIES	1	2	3	4	5	6	7	8	9	10	11	12	13	14	15
1. Play with children		x	x		x	x	x								
2. Paint	x		x	x	x		x								
3. Read a book	x					x									
4. Watch a movie					x										
5. Talk to friends	x		x												
6. Garden		x													
7. Collect shells							x								
8. Take a walk							x								
9. Shop			x												
10. Camp															
11. Sightsee						x									
12. Go to a museum						x									
13. Play with dog		x	x		x										
14. Get a massage	x														
15.															
16.															
17.															
18.															
19.															
20															
21															
22															
23															

Beck's Cognitive Distortions

Personalizing is assuming that an activating event is targeted toward you specifically. *Do others always know what you are thinking?*

Catastrophizing/Magnifying assuming there is more importance to an activating event that is unrealistic. *Have you always excelled before?*

Polarized Thinking Assuming that an event only has two possible meanings, failure to pay attention to nuances. *When others come in second, third or last does that make them losers? Why are you a loser if you don't come in first?*

Selective Abstraction assuming that one extracted part of an event applies to the whole event. *What have people said about the total event?*

Overgeneralizing assuming that one experience represents all experiences or events. *What happened at other events?*

Arbitrary Inference assuming there is meaning to an event when there is no evidence to support that meaning. *How do you know what others are thinking? Have there been times when your meaning was misunderstood?*

Unrealistic Expectations having expectations of yourself and others that are not supported by evidence. *How do you know what others want without them telling you?*

ASSIGNMENT VII
PART 1

Do you see similarities between Beck's cognitive distortions? What are they? Go to the negative thoughts example and assign one of Beck's Cognitive Distortions to each of them.

Cognitive restructuring is used to change your irrational thoughts. Four major techniques are used. (1) logical disputation questions (*to examine the logical uniformity of your beliefs.* (2) reality testing tolerance *(Where is the evidence?)* (3) Pragmatic disputation question (*evaluating the hedonistic value - pain or pleasure?)* **(4)** relaxation.

ASSIGNMENT VII
PART 2

Take each of your thoughts from your baseline and argue with yourself about them. Sometimes there is more to the whole belief than is just beneath the surface issue. What is the underlying thought?

There are five ways of dealing with activating events: (1) Don't respond to them (2) Avoid them (3) Change them (4) Cope with them (5) Change the way we respond to them (CBT)

ASSIGNMENT VIII

Select a negative thought from the negative thoughts list. State the thought and the correlating feeling. Next change the negative thought to a positive thought and the correlating feeling.

RELAXATION

By now you are probably tense and anxious. Remember the breathing and visualizing that we talked about earlier in Assignment IV. Use these simple techniques to relax. Use them anytime you are tense or stressed. They will often help you find that elusive solution that seemed to be just out of reach.

Another Relaxation exercise that you can do anywhere (in the car, at a stop sign, at work, etc.) is this: Let your arms relax down at your sides. Imagine all your negative thoughts and feelings are thick black tar-like goo. They are oozing up through your legs, up through your body, down from your head. They ooze down your arm and out through your finger tips and drip onto the floor. Mentally sweep them away or symbolically open you car door and let them flow out onto the street.

This breathing exercise is called the 4-4-4 breathing. Inhale through your nose slowly to the count of four (4), hold the breath for the count of four (4) and let it out slowly to the count of four.

Muscle Relaxation

Find a quiet place for this exercise. You can sit or lie down, but get comfortable. Close your eyes. Be aware of the tensions and feeling of relaxations in your body as you do this exercise.

Make a fist with you right hand as tightly as you can. Hold it for a few seconds, then open your and relax it. Repeat this with your right hand again. Repeat this part with your left hand. Bend your elbows and flex your biceps. Hold it for a few seconds and then relax your arms, letting them hang at your side. Repeat this one more time. Wrinkle your forehead as tightly as you can. Relax and let your forehead smooth out (notice that your forehead and scalp both relax.). Now frown and hold it for a second (your forehead will tighten). Relax and allow your forehead to smooth out.

With your eyes closed, squint your eyes very tightly. Relax. Repeat. Clench your jaw tightly. Relax. (Your mouth will be slightly open) Repeat. Press your tongue against the roof of your mouth. Relax. Repeat. Purse your lip together. Relax. Repeat.

Move your head back as far as it can go. Roll it to your right and then to your left. Bring your head forward and down toward your chest. Now relax and allow your shoulders to return to a comfortable position. Repeat. Shrug your shoulders and hunch your head down between them. Relax your shoulders and allow them to return to a relaxed position.

Tighten your stomach and hold. Relax your stomach. Put your hand on your stomach and breathe in pushing your stomach against your hand. Relax. Arch your back. Relax.

Tighten your buttock and thighs. Tighten your thighs by pressing down hard with your heels. Relax. Repeat. Curl your toes down causing your calves to tighten. Relax. Repeat. Bend your toes toward your head, causing tension in your shins. Relax. Repeat.

References:

Anthony, M. M., Beiling, P.J. and McCabe, R.E. (2006). Cognitive-behavioral therapy in groups. The Guildford Press. New York, NY.

Burns, Ed, Phd. (2007 - 2008). Professor CBT class lectures. Eastern Washington University. School of Social Work. Cheney, WA.

Cahill, S.P. Foa, E.B. and Riggs, D.S. (2006). Prolonged Exposure treatment of post-traumatic stress disorders. U.M. Fallette and J.I. Ruzek (Eds). Cognitive-behavioral therapies for trauma (2nd Ed). The Guildford Press. New York, NY.

De Jong, P. (2002). Solution-focus therapy. Greene, GJ. And Roberts, A.R. (Eds) Social workers desk reference. Oxford University Press. Orlando, Fl.

Donohue, W.T. and Fisher, J.E. (Eds). (2006). Practitioners Guide to evidence-based psycho therapy. Springer. New York, NY.

Early, T.J. and Vonk, M.E. (2002). Cognitive-behavioral therapy. Greene, G. and Roberts, A.R. (Eds) Social workers desk reference. Oxford University Press. Orlando, Fl.

Kelly, P. (2002). Narrative therapy. Greene, G.J. and Roberts, A.R. (Eds) Social Worker's desk reference. Oxford University Press. Orlando, Fl.

Leahy, R.L. (2006). Cognitive Therapy techniques: A practitioner's guide. The Guildford Press. New York, NY.

Linehan, M.M. and Wagner A.W. (2002). Applications of dialectical behavior therapy to post traumatic stress disorder and related problems. Fallette, V.M. and Ruzek, J.I. (Eds). Cognitive-behavioral therapies for trauma. (2nd Ed.). The Guildford Press. New York, NY.

McMullin, R.E. (2000). Handbook of cognitive therapy techniques. WW Norton and Company, Inc. New York, NY.

NACBT Online Headquarters, National Association of Cognitive-behavioral

Therapists (2007). Accessed 8 May 2007 from
http//ww.nacbt.org/whatiscbt.htm.

Resick, A.E., Shipherd, J.C. and Street, A. E. (2006), Cognitive therapy for post-
traumatic stress disorder. Cognitive-behavior therapy for trauma (2nd Ed.).
The Guildford Press. New York, NY.

Rubin, A. (2002). Eye movement desensitization and reprocessing. Greene, G.J.
and Roberts, A.R. (Eds) Social worker's desk reference. Oxford University
Press. Orlando, Fl.

www.ingramcontent.com/pod-product-compliance
Lightning Source LLC
Chambersburg PA
CBHW081810280526
45789CB00008B/3075